the PET -to- GET

SNAKE

ROB COLSON

WAYLAND

Published in paperback in 201... [redacted]
Copyright © Hodder and Stou... [redacted]

Wayland
An imprint of
Hachette Children's Group
Part of Hodder & Stoughton
Carmelite House
50 Victoria Embankment
London EC4Y 0DZ

All Rights Reserved.
Editor: Annabel Stones

Produced for Wayland by
Tall Tree Ltd
Consultant: Jane Hallam

ISBN 978 0 7502 8933 7
Dewey number: 639.3'96-dc23
10 9 8 7 6 5 4 3 2 1
Printed in China

MIX
Paper from
responsible sources
FSC® C104740
FSC
www.fsc.org

Wayland is a division of Hachette Children's
Books, an Hachette UK company
www.hachette.co.uk

The publisher would would like to thank the following for
their kind permission to reproduce their photographs:

Key: (t) top; (c) centre; (b) bottom; (l) left; (r) right
(Shutterstock.com unless stated otherwise)

Front cover, back cover Isselee/Dreamstime.com, 1
Michiel de Wit, 2 Eric Isselee, 4 Rebecca Abell, 5t, 5b, 6
Eric Isselee, 7t lunatic67, 7b Skynavin, 8l Dreamstime.
com, 8-9 Isselee/Dreamstime.com, 9 John Cancalosi/
Gettyimages, 10l L Kennedy/Alamy, 11t Eric Isselee, 11b
leapdogcommunications, 12-13 Heidi & Hans-Jurgen
Koch/Gettyimages, 12bl Exo-Terra, 12br Gina Kelly/Alamy,
13 Ryan Kelm, 14-15 BogdanBoev, 15 Jason Patrick Ross,
16 Ehrman Photographic, 17t 20 below photography, 17b
Heiko Kiera, 18t Gerald A. DeBoer, 18-19 Bruce MacQueen,
19t Steve Jurvetson/CC Attribution, 20 Brenda Carson, 21t
Matt Jeppson, 21b Rui Ferreira, 22b Eric Isselee, 22-23,
23t fivespots, 24b Gina Kelly/Alamy, 24-25 AppStock, 26-27
Matt Jeppson, 27t Marek Velechovsky, 27b Norman
Benton/CC Attribution Sharealike, 28bl Erik Freeland/
Corbis, 28-29 Matt Jeppson, 29c Alberto Loyo, 29b
Heiko Kiera, 30tl Isselee/Dreamstime.com, 30tcl Skynavin,
30tcr Norman Benton/CC Attribution Sharealike, 30tr
fivespots, 30b lunatic67

CONTENTS

WHY A SNAKE?

Have you always been fascinated by snakes? Do they make you nervous, or do you wonder why people are so scared of them? Keeping a snake will probably divide your family and friends – some will love handling it as much as you do, but others may stay well away.

You will need to get to know your snake before you handle it. When you do, you will feel its strong muscles as it moves.

WHAT ARE SNAKES?

Snakes are **reptiles**. These are a group of animals that have scaly skin and are **cold-blooded**. Most reptiles have legs, but snakes don't. Instead, they slither along by rippling their muscular bodies. They also have no eyelids or external ears. Snakes are **solitary** animals and **carnivores** that hunt other animals to eat.

THINK FIRST

Keeping a snake is a big commitment. Before you buy a snake, discuss it with your family and be sure to consider the pros and cons. Snakes are beautiful creatures that make fascinating pets, but you'll need to keep it safe. Snakes are good at escaping from their homes, and your family may need reassurance that it won't get out of its cage.

Snakes are always sticking their tongues out. They're not being rude – snakes don't have noses, so they 'smell' the air with their tongues instead.

Snakes have stretchy jaws that can open very wide and swallow large prey. This python is swallowing a rat head first.

WHICH SNAKE?

When choosing a snake, you need to consider how large it is going to become. Snakes keep growing throughout their lives and it is best not to keep **species** that grow very big. Don't choose **venomous** snakes or snakes that grow so large that they become dangerous to people.

A baby milk snake emerges from its egg.

AT THE BREEDER'S

It is best to buy a **captive-bred** snake from a reptile **breeder**. Ask the breeder to show you the snake's eating and shedding records. The breeder is also an excellent person to ask any questions you may have about keeping snakes. Ideally you should buy a young snake as it will get used to you more easily and you get to watch it grow up.

Snakes start life as eggs. The female may lay between five and 50 eggs, which hatch after a few weeks. The young snakes are independent as soon as they hatch and are not cared for by their mothers.

CONSTRICTORS

Most of the snakes people keep as pets are constrictors. In the wild, constrictors kill their **prey** by squeezing it to death. Small constrictors are no danger to anything larger than a mouse, but large ones, such as some pythons, can grow to more than 3 metres long and may be dangerous to larger animals and even people. Do not buy a large constrictor as a first pet.

The green tree boa is a constrictor that grows up to 2 metres long. It can be kept as a pet, but it is best to gain experience with a smaller snake first.

A HEALTHY SNAKE

Make sure that the snake you choose is alert and flicks out its tongue when you come near. It should be curious to get a good smell of you. It should have bright, shiny skin and there should be no cuts or scrapes on its body. Its body should be well-rounded and you should not be able to see any of its backbones.

Snakes such as cobras kill their prey by injecting venom into them with their fangs. You should not keep venomous snakes as pets.

CORN SNAKE
FACTFILE

Corn snakes are ideal first snakes. They can be handled regularly and, unlike some other constrictors, they won't grow too big.

FEEDING

Feed a young snake **pinkies** every 5–6 days. Move on to larger mice as it grows, feeding it once every couple of weeks. Very large corn snakes may need two mice or a larger rat. Place the food on a rock or stone, not in the **substrate** (see page 11), to make sure that the snake does not eat any substrate along with the mouse.

Markings help to **camouflage** snakes in the wild.

HIBERNATION

Your corn snake will probably stop feeding and **hibernate** through the winter. Be sure to switch off its heat pad while it sleeps.

IN THE WILD

Corn snakes are native to southeastern **USA**, where they live in farmland and pine forest. They are often found in corn stores, where they feed on the mice and rats that eat the corn. This is where their name comes from. Corn snakes are popular with farmers as they help with pest control by eating **rodents**.

HANDLING

Corn snakes can be handled regularly, and enjoy the opportunity to come out of their vivarium for a while. Handle your corn snake for 10–15 minutes three or four times a week.

VIVARIUM

Corn snakes are not highly active, so they don't need a huge **vivarium** (see page 10). The temperature range should be 21–30°C. Place one hide at the cool end of the vivarium and another at the warm end. You should add branches for the snake to climb.

Corn snakes have orange and black markings on their backs, and striking black and white chequered bellies.

SNAKE HOUSE

Your snake will need a secure cage called a vivarium to live in. You can use a fish tank, but the opening must be securely fastened to stop your snake from escaping. The tank should be large enough for the snake to stretch out straight and to turn around easily.

WARM AND COOL

Snakes are cold-blooded, which means that they need a warm place to give them energy. Heat the vivarium using a heat pad or a ceramic bulb, but make sure that the snake cannot directly touch the heat source. Place the heater at one end of the vivarium. This will provide a **heat gradient** between a hot end and a cool end. Your snake will **bask** at the hot end. When it gets too hot, it will retreat to the cool end, where it will curl up and rest.

Your snake will try to get out of its tank, so make sure that all the doors are securely fastened. Remember that snakes have strong muscles and will force open any weak spot.

FURNITURE

Place rocks and branches around the vivarium. You can also use plastic plants to make your snake feel at home. A hard rock is essential for the snake to rub against when shedding its skin. When they are resting, snakes like to feel safe and secure, so you must give them hiding places. You can buy hides or make them yourself from upside-down plant pots.

SUBSTRATE

Cover the bottom of the vivarium with substrate – a loose material such as pine wood shavings. You can buy this from a pet shop. It will give your snake something soft to lie on that will feel like soil. Never use cedar wood shavings as these are poisonous to snakes.

In the wild, even fierce snakes such as this rattlesnake like to feel safe curled up underneath a rock.

Rattlesnakes are venomous, and should only be kept by experts.

CLEAN AND HEALTHY

The best way to make your snake happy is to keep its vivarium tidy. Remove droppings when you see them, change the water daily and every few weeks give it a good clean.

FRESH TANK

When you clean the vivarium, place the snake in a plastic container with breathing holes. Take everything out and wash it, rinsing with water. Allow the vivarium to dry and replace the substrate before returning the snake.

When you put the furniture back in the tank, change it around a bit. Your snake will enjoy exploring its new surroundings and this will stop it from becoming bored.

Snakes need a fresh supply of water. Use a heavy water bowl that the snake won't knock over.

SHEDDING

Snakes must shed their skin in order to grow. They do this several times a year. Shortly before it sheds, you will notice your snake's skin become dull and its eyes turn a bluish-grey colour. It may refuse food and back away if you try to handle it. When it is ready to shed, it first rubs its head against a rock and works its head free of the old skin. It then slithers out of the skin, often leaving the whole thing in one piece.

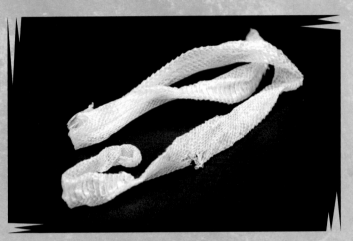

Remove the old skin from the vivarium as soon as you see it.

SKIN RECORD

Often a snake manages to shed its skin in one whole piece. You can keep the old skins and label them with the date of the shed. The size of the skins will form a record of your snake's growth over the years. Looking back at its skins, you won't believe how small your snake used to be!

This rat snake is starting to shed its old skin.

GREY RAT SNAKE
FACTFILE

Grey rat snakes are tree-dwelling constrictors. Like corn snakes, they are great escape artists and they are also good climbers. As their name suggests, their favourite food in the wild is the rat, but they will eat any prey that is small enough to swallow.

Lifespan:
up to 18 years

Food in the wild:
Mice, rats, small birds, bird eggs

Maximum Length:
2 metres

Ease of care: Easy

Scales on the belly and around the mouth are off-white.

IN THE WILD

Grey rat snakes are found in central and eastern parts of North America, from the Gulf of Mexico in the south to Ontario, Canada, in the north. They live in forests and along tree-lined rivers and streams.

FOOD

Feed rat snakes a mouse every 7–10 days. They eat the same food as their cousin the corn snake.

This grey rat snake lives in the lush forests of Alabama.

VIVARIUM

Grey rat snakes are closely related to corn snakes, and need a similar temperature range of 21–30°C. They often hunt in trees in the wild, so it is important to have a vivarium that is quite tall. Provide plenty of branches reaching up through the vivarium for your snake to climb.

HIBERNATION

If you keep them warm, rat snakes may not hibernate, but if your snake refuses food in the autumn, reduce the temperature so that it can slow down for the winter.

DINNER TIME

Watching snakes eat is fascinating. You should feed your snake dead mice, which you can buy from a pet shop. Never feed them live mice. Keep the mice in the freezer and thaw them out one at a time when needed.

Snakes swallow their prey whole.

HOW BIG?

Feed your snake mice that are about 1.5 times as wide as the snake's body. Immediately after the snake has eaten, you should be able to see a noticeable lump inside it where the mouse is. If there is no obvious lump, it is time to move up to a bigger mouse.

It is hard to believe such a large mouse can fit inside such a small mouth.

FEEDING BY HAND
You will never see your snake move as quickly as it does when it grabs its prey! The snake may mistake your fingers for food, so hold the mouse by its tail with a pair of tongs. If it does not take the food straight away, jiggle the mouse around until the snake strikes. Then you can watch as the snake swallows the mouse whole. If the snake will not take the mouse directly from you, leave it on a rock and come back later to check. Some snakes prefer to eat in private.

In the wild, snakes will eat anything that's the right size. This garter snake is swallowing a frog head first.

DON'T OVERFEED
Younger snakes should be fed every few days, while adults should eat every 7–10 days, depending on the species. Snakes will eat too much if you let them, so don't be tempted to feed your snake more often than this as it will get fat.

Baby snakes are ready to hunt as soon as they hatch.

GARTER SNAKE
FACTFILE

Very small baby garter snakes can be fed on worms or even slugs.

Garter snakes are a group of thin, fast-moving snakes that do not grow very large. They are easy to keep, but may not like regular handling.

Lifespan:
up to 20 years

Food in the wild:
Slugs, worms, frogs, lizards

Maximum Length:
1 metre

Ease of care: Easy

FOOD

Larger garter snakes will eat small mice, and these give them all the nutrients they need. Young snakes may not want mice or may be too small to swallow a pinkie. Try small snakes on pieces of cut-up pinkie. They may not be interested, in which case, you may have to feed your snake with fish or live worms. As the snake grows, it should start taking mice instead, and when it does, stop feeding it anything else.

IN THE WILD

Garter snakes are widespread across North America. The common garter snake is the only species found in Alaska, where it is too cold for other snakes. They often live near water, feeding on frogs, salamanders and even tadpoles, but will eat anything they can catch.

The coast garter snake lives in the northeast states of the USA.

VIVARIUM

Garter snakes do not need large vivariums. In fact, if the vivarium is too large, they will feel stressed. A vivarium that is about twice the length of the snake is about right. Provide a temperature range of 22–30°C. When they get too hot, garter snakes like to bathe in water, so make sure the water bowl is large enough for it to curl up in.

A common garter snake has a yellow belly and brown back.

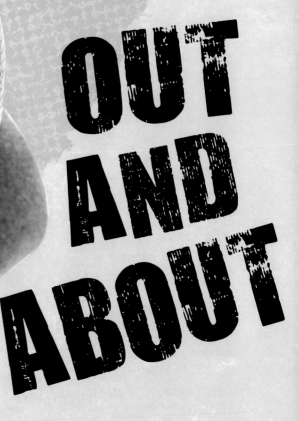

OUT AND ABOUT

Snakes are curious animals. They can enjoy being handled as it gives them an opportunity to come out of their vivarium and explore some new surroundings. By handling your snake, you'll get to know it as an individual. Every snake has its own personality.

When you handle your snake, make sure you support its body so that it feels safe. Never handle a snake soon after feeding it, as it may throw up its meal.

MAKING FRIENDS

Before you pick up your snake, it will need to get used to you touching it. Start by stroking it in its vivarium. Move slowly and remember that to the snake you are a giant. When you do pick the snake up, hold it gently behind the head with one hand and support its body with the other. Hold it firmly as this will make the snake feel safe.

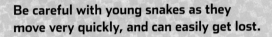

Be careful with young snakes as they move very quickly, and can easily get lost.

Snakes wrap their bodies around arms to feel more secure.

CURIOUS SNAKE

Your snake will explore your clothes, and may even try to get into your pockets. If it is constantly trying to get away, this means that it has had enough of being handled. Even if it is not trying to get away, put it back in its vivarium after about 15 minutes.

SLOWING DOWN FOR WINTER

In the autumn, your snake may refuse to eat. The shortening days have told it that it will soon be time to hibernate for the winter. In preparation, it clears all the food out of its system. This process is called **brumation**. When it happens, you will need to gradually reduce the temperature in the vivarium. This slows down the snake's body processes so that it doesn't waste energy. A snake may hibernate for three or four months through winter. Turn the heater back on in spring, and the snake will slowly wake up and be ready to eat again.

BALL PYTHON
FACTFILE

Lifespan:
up to 40 years

Food in the wild:
Mice, birds, amphibians

Maximum Length:
1.5 metres (females grow larger than males)

Ease of care: Easy

Ball pythons, also known as royal pythons, are a very popular choice for snake keepers. They are good-natured and easy to look after, but think carefully before buying one as they live for a long time.

HANDLING

Ball pythons are quite slow-moving and even clumsy compared to other snakes. They are easy to handle, but only take them out of their vivarium for a few minutes at a time.

CAPTIVE IS BEST

It is very important to buy a ball python from a breeder who has bred it in captivity. Many ball pythons are captured in the wild to be sold as pets, but wild snakes often do not like to be kept in vivariums. A captive-bred snake will be much happier to live with you and easier to look after.

This ball python has been bred in captivity. Its breeder will have a record of where and when it was born.

FOOD

As with other constrictors, feed your ball python dead mice. Ball pythons regularly go on fasts for no obvious reason, so do not worry if your snake refuses food occasionally. Just come back a week later and try again.

VIVARIUM

Provide a medium-sized vivarium that is about one-third the snake's length in height. The temperature should range from **26–33°C**, with hides at both the warm and the cool end.

This bumble bee ball python is warming itself on a sunny rock.

IN THE WILD

Ball pythons live in grasslands in Central Africa. During hot, dry weather, they hide in burrows and go into **aestivation**, a sleep-like state similar to hibernation, but in response to heat rather than cold.

This species is called a black pewter ball python.

23

HEALTH CHECK

Snakes rarely get ill, but you should give your snake a quick check each time you handle it to make sure it is healthy. Remember to wash your hands after handling the snake as its skin may carry germs.

OFF ITS FOOD

The most common problems occur at feeding time. A snake can stop eating for a variety of reasons: it may be getting ready to shed its skin, preparing for hibernation or just bored with eating the same thing all the time. Do not worry if your snake refuses food occasionally. This is only a cause for concern if it is starting to behave differently and looks in bad condition. If the problem continues for more than a few weeks, take it to the vet.

SHEDDING PROBLEMS

If you notice some old skin stuck to your snake, it may need some help to get rid of it. Place a bowl of warm water in the vivarium. The snake will bathe in the water, and this will help it to finish shedding its old skin. Do not try to pull the skin off yourself.

Snakes bathe in water to help them shed old skin, and also simply to cool down.

DANGER SIGNS

Look out for the following things when you check your snake:

- Has it lost interest in food?
- Is it less active than usual?
- Does its skin look wrinkly or dull in colour?
- Is it losing weight?
- Are there any bumps on its skin?

WASH YOUR HANDS

Snake skin sometimes carries the germ **salmonella**. You should always wash your hands after handling a snake to get rid of any germs.

SNAKE BITES

If it gets scared, your snake may bite you. Don't panic. The bites of constrictors are not venomous. Wait for the snake to let go, clean any cuts with antiseptic cream and tell an adult what has happened.

MILK SNAKE
FACTFILE

Milk snakes are attractive snakes with striking bands of colours around their bodies. They can be handled regularly and are a good choice as a pet.

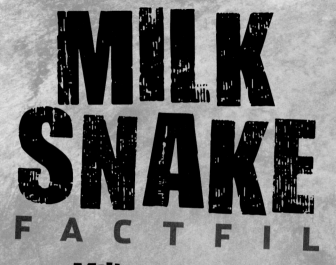

Lifespan:
15–20 years

Food in the wild:
Mice, birds, amphibians

Maximum Length:
2 metres

Ease of care:
Medium

VIVARIUM
Give your snake a medium-sized vivarium with a temperature range of 24–30°C. Provide two hides – one at the cool end and the other at the warm end.

IN THE WILD

Milk snakes are found across North America and Central America. They will eat any small animal, but mostly feed on rodents, hunting at night.

This young milk snake is eating a pinkie.

FOOD

Like other constrictors, milk snakes should be fed dead mice. Adult snakes can also be fed day-old chicks to give their diet some variety.

DEADLY DOUBLE

Milk snakes have a clever way to stay safe in the wild. They are coloured with bands of red, black and yellow, which makes them look very similar to the coral snake, which is venomous. However, the colours are in a different order. On the deadly coral snake, the red band touches yellow, while on the milk snake, the red bands are next to black. **Predators** cannot tell the difference, though, and stay away.

This snake's red bands touch yellow, which means that it is a venomous coral snake. Coral snakes should never be kept as pets.

SAYING GOODBYE

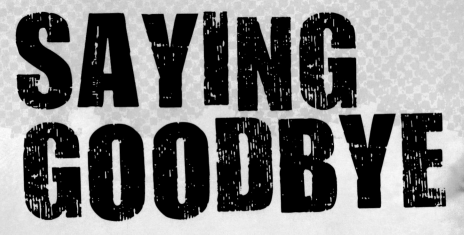

As snakes get older, they tend to slow down, rest more and eat less often. Snakes live long lives, but like all living creatures, they will die one day. This will be a sad day, but remember that your snake had a happy life.

When you first get your snake, it is a good idea to take it to the vet. The vet will give it a thorough examination and any treatment it might need. With a bit of luck, you will not be back at the vet's for a long time.

MISSING YOUR FRIEND

You may feel sad when your snake dies. But it will get easier with time, and eventually you will be able to think back to your time together and smile. You may decide you want to keep another snake, which will be a whole new adventure.

AMAZING SNAKE FACTS

The giant green anaconda (left) lives in the forests of South America. It can grow to more than 6 metres in length.

Sea snakes live in coastal waters in tropical oceans. They have a flattened body to help them to swim, and spend their whole lives in water.

Rattlesnakes have rattles in their tails to scare off predators. The rattle is made from hollow segments. Each time the snake sheds its skin, a new segment is added to its rattle.

This corn snake has grown near to its maximum size. It has slowed down a lot since it was young, and eats less often.

KEEPING A RECORD

A great way to remember your snake when it is gone is to keep a record. This could be a scrapbook or a webpage. Keep photos of your snake and even its old skins in a scrapbook, and these will tell the story of the snake's life.

SNAKE QUIZ

Test your snake knowledge with this short quiz.

Can you identify these four snakes from their photos?

1.

2.

3.

4.

5. How did the corn snake get its name?

6. How does a constrictor kill its prey?

7. Why should you wash your hands after handling a snake?

8. Where do ball pythons live in the wild?

9. If a snake has bands of red next to bands of yellow on its body, is it venomous?

10. If a snake's eyes turn bluish-grey, what is about to happen?

ANSWERS
1. Corn snake
2. Cobra
3. Coral snake
4. Ball python
5. It likes to hunt rats around corn stores.
6. It squeezes it to death.
7. The skin can carry the germ salmonella.
8. In Central Africa.
9. Yes, it is a coral snake.
10. It is about to shed its skin.

GLOSSARY

AESTIVATION
A sleep-like state that some animals enter into to save energy and water when the weather is very hot and dry.

BASK
To lie in a hot place in order to warm up.

BREEDER
A person who keeps animals in order to produce young.

BRUMATION
A period during which a snake stops eating just before it goes into hibernation.

CAMOUFLAGE
The use of colour and shape to blend in with the background. Snakes use camouflage to hide from predators and prey.

CAPTIVE-BREEDING
The breeding of animals from parents that are being cared for by humans. You should only buy captive-bred snakes.

CARNIVORE
An animal that eats other animals.

COLD-BLOODED
Lacking the ability to keep a constant body temperature. Animals that are cold-blooded, such as snakes, warm up in the sun to give them energy.

HEAT GRADIENT
The temperature difference between the hot end of a vivarium and the cool end.

HIBERNATION
A sleep-like state that some animals enter into to save energy during the winter.

MAMMAL
A warm-blooded animal that has hair when it is young and feeds its babies with milk.

NUTRIENTS
Chemicals in food that are essential to keep an animal healthy.

PINKIE
A small, hairless mouse that snakes eat. Pinkies are bought frozen from pet shops, and thawed out before they are fed to the snake.

PREDATOR
An animal that hunts and kills other animals to eat.

PREY
An animal that is hunted and killed by other animals.

REPTILE
A group of animals that includes snakes and lizards. Reptiles are cold-blooded and have scaly skin.

RODENT
A group of mammals that includes mice, rats and beavers. Rodents have four large front teeth that they use to gnaw on things.

SALMONELLA
A germ sometimes found on snake skin that causes fever and stomach pain.

SOLITARY
Living alone. Solitary animals spend most of their lives on their own and don't get lonely.

SPECIES
A kind of living thing. Members of the same species are able to reproduce with one another.

SUBSTRATE
The soft, loose material at the bottom of a vivarium.

VENOMOUS
Possessing a bite or sting that contains venom. Some snakes have a venomous bite. The venom is injected into the body of the snake's victim and makes it ill.

VIVARIUM
A special cage to house a snake, in which conditions are similar to those it would experience in the wild.

USEFUL WEBSITES

www.thebhs.org
Website of the British Herpetological Society, devoted to reptiles and amphibians. Includes the Young Herpetologists Club for young people mad about reptiles.

www.nhm.ac.uk
Website of the Natural History Museum in London, with lots of information about all kinds of animals. Learn about how snakes live in the wild.

INDEX